THRIFT STORE HUSTLE

EASILY MAKE $1000+ A MONTH PROFIT BUYING ITEMS FROM THRIFT STORES

BY ETHAN FROST

Introduction

Welcome to Thrift Store Hustle. In this book, I will show you the strategies and methods you need to make $1,000 profit per month from thrift stores. I have used these methods over the past few years to provide a great part-time income for myself and my family.

There are many thrift stores all across America to find items to sell. There are also other sources, such as garage sales and flea markets. These all can be used as awesome sources to make your $1,000 a month profit. In this book, I will show you a consistent method and routine to make $1,000 a month.

As you set up your system, which consists of finding profitable items selling them to customers, you will profit. There are some people that are even able to make a full-time income selling items from thrift stores and from similar places. In order to do that though, it takes considerable skill and dedication as well as much learning.

This book is for both beginners as well as those that may have been sourcing items from thrift stores for quite some time. This book his great nuggets to help just about anyone looking to start or continue to profit.

Section 1. Thrift Stores Overview

Thrift stores sell used items for the most part. Although sometimes they have many items that are unopened and brand new. Most of the items within the store are donations from people or businesses around the area and in the community. These items are for the most part reasonably priced and way below what you would pay for the same item brand new in retail stores.

The thrift store proceeds often go to a worthwhile cause to help others. With each store having a particular mission that it focuses on, which is pretty cool.

So how does making money from thrift stores work in your case?

Items that are priced by thrift store workers are usually priced quite low. This is because the thrift store needs to sell the items within a particular time frame before they get more stock.

The thing is, a particular thrift store only reaches a certain amount of people in a small area in general. It is just a small store in a particular physical location. There are many people across America as well as globally, that might be looking for the items that you could find in a particular physical thrift store. They are willing to pay much more than the thrift store is selling it for.

For instance, you might find a particular used DVD in a thrift store. The thrift store might be selling it to a few dozen people that might come across it on the shelf. None of them might be particularly interested in it and pass it by in the thrift store.

The thrift store tries to sell it for $1.99, and it doesn't sell. If you were to sell that same DVD online, there is such a wider audience across the world that can bid or purchase the DVD. You might be able to sell it for $35. There are millions upon millions of people that shop online. With the good likelihood that you might be able to get that price for it.

So the key is to consistently buy items in demand with a good resale value from thrift stores. This will take a good feel and understanding if particular items will sell at a high price on the internet. The better you get at spotting good deals (buy low at thrifts and sell high online) the more profit you can potentially make.

Types of Thrifts

There are many popular thrift stores that are known nationwide. Stores such as Goodwill, Salvation Army, and Savers will be the bread and butter of your thrifting program.

This is because they are very popular and receive many of the best donations. They also get donations often and rotate their stock frequently. Their prices might be a bit higher than many other thrift stores, but it won't matter because they have items that usually can get you more profits if you decide to resell them online.

Over the last couple of years, Goodwill and a few other thrift stores have also begun to sell some of their items online. This means that you will have to move quickly and start to get your practicing in, in terms of thrifting. You're going to have to learn what you're looking for so you can be smart when purchasing. Just because some thrift stores are selling online doesn't mean that there aren't still many great finds which you can make a profit from.

There are also other small mom and pop, hole in the wall type thrift stores in your area They will usually not be as organized or efficient in how they handle their goods. So steals, deals and prices may be really remarkable. These thrifts will also be a good source of income.

Similar Sources

Although this book is about making money from thrift stores, I will also let you know you can find great products at places that are just like thrift stores. One option of these is garage sales. Garage sales are held usually on weekends and consist of items that people no longer want in their homes.

They sell these items for pretty good prices for the most part. The good news is that garage sales can sometimes have some great gems. The owners might be selling them dirt cheap, even cheaper than thrift stores. Sometimes they have very rare items and expensive items that they are selling without real knowledge of their worth.

You can sometimes buy things in bulk, such as whole collections of books or whole collections of action figures which will be very cheap if you buy them as a collection. You usually can't do this at thrift stores.

The bad news is that garage sales can be hit-or-miss. If you have any experience with garage sales you might know that sometimes it's just junk that people don't want in their house and they're trying to get rid of it. So it basically it depends on the quality of what they're selling.

Other good sources are rummage sales and flea markets. These are some great options because there are quite a few sellers in one place. If just a few are selling some great items, it will be well worth it. Always remember to come earlier to a sale. This will help you get the best deals early.

Section 2. Where Will I Sell Thrift Store Items?

If you buy a whole bunch of things at a thrift store where would you sell them? This book will teach you the two main places to make income selling thrift store items. Those two main places are eBay and Amazon.

Sure, there are other places online to sell your thrift store finds. The problem is they don't have as much traffic as these two selling platforms. Time is very important because you probably have a full-time job? What I'm trying to teach you is the quickest and most efficient way to profit and anything that might slow you down or not get you to your goal of $1,000 a month will not be taught here for the most part.

eBay has been around for quite some time. A few years ago eBay was at its peak and people were really profiting big time from the idea of selling items online. Today eBay is still a wonderful place to make money by selling used items or even items that are brand new that you got cheaply.

It isn't as profitable as it used to be but if you are smart you can make a great profit. You may already have an eBay account and you may have sold things already on the eBay platform. What you're going to want to do is set up and get an account if you don't have one. eBay maybe where you sell most of your thrift store items. Amazon.com is the premier website for buying things on the internet. The good news is that you can sell things for much higher on Amazon that you can on eBay. The bad news is that

Amazon is a lot more strict than eBay. There are limitations and restrictions on what you can and cannot sell on Amazon.

It may be too much of a task to try to explain everything about what you can and can't sell on Amazon in this book. Instead, I will give a good quick overview of it for you. On Amazon.com you can sell books and media products, as well as toys and board games for example. W

hen you sell the items on Amazon they usually must be in good condition, and not everything can be sold in used condition. For instance, baby products cannot be sold on Amazon if they are not brand new. Used clothing cannot be sold on Amazon either. You also must be approved in quite a few categories to sell on Amazon. You cannot sell clothes or grocery items on Amazon without approval.

The good news is what you CAN sell on Amazon will bring you much much more than what you will sell on eBay. The top things I have sold on Amazon from thrift stores are books, CDs, DVDs, board games, VHS, and many other bric-a-brac type items.

Both Amazon and eBay charge fees if you want to sell on their platform. You will be advertising your product on their platform so they will charge you a fee. Amazon charges a bit more than eBay, but that's okay because Amazon reaches many more people. Plus You can sell your items for way more on Amazon. eBay charges fees as well.

There may be other places you can sell your thrift store items. I won't go over them because they aren't as profitable as Amazon and eBay. As you get good at selling on these two platforms you might want to branch out to find some other places to sell your items. Just know that they won't be as lucrative for the most part.

Section 3. What Do I buy?

If you have been in a thrift store before you might have a good idea about what they sell, which is just about anything you might find an American household.

The good thing is that in thrift stores their different sections. This will help you see that each section of a thrift store has different possibilities for you. You may not want to sell everything and every type of item that thrift stores have. For instance, although I have sold some clothing from thrift stores on eBay, I almost always skip over clothing that I see. The reason for this is I'm not particularly that interested in selling clothes.

There are some people on eBay that make hundreds of dollars a month or more selling clothes. So it isn't bad or good to sell or not to sell clothes it just depends on what you want to focus on. My advice is to find something or group of items that thrift stores carry that you can focus on.

You might want to focus on selling books. You might want to focus selling shoes. You might want to look into selling Electronics. What you're going to need to do is really get good at 2 or 3 different categories.

Okay, so you might have an idea of what you might want to start selling. You're going to have to learn if an item you find in a thrift store is going to make you a good profit or not.

You will need an Amazon scanning app on your phone or an eBay app. When you find an item on the shelf and thrift store the first thing you'll do is look at the price. Sometimes thrift stores price an item too high. Even though it might be a good item, because they priced it too high you won't be able to make a profit on it by selling it online.

For instance, you might find a children's DVD that is priced at $9.99 which is pretty high for a thrift store price. It might be selling for $16 on amazon.com. It won't be a good idea to purchase it. That is because if you buy it for about $10 then figuring your cost to ship it. Plus Amazon fees you have to pay Amazon in order to sell your product on their platform. You will actually not make any Money. If children's DVD was selling for $2 it would probably be a great buy because after spending for purchasing, Amazon fees, and your costs to ship it to your customer you will make a pretty good profit.

A tip that I would give you is find something that you know is worth a lot. you may also want to start with a category that you are familiar with already. Then look it up on your Amazon app or your eBay app and see what it's selling for.

If you see that your hunch was right and it's selling for a lot more than the thrift store is selling it for, purchase it. Do this with a dozen or so items. You will then list these items and get your thrift game and system started.

Apps

The two apps I recommend to check prices on Amazon are Profit Bandit app and the Amazon app. The Amazon App is free. The Profit Bandit app will cost about $10 a month.

The app that you would use for eBay is the eBay app which is free.

Profit Calculator

Amazon has a profit calculator. You're going to want to go and buy items at a low price and sell them at a high price on Amazon. This Amazon profit calculator which is free is a very important tool. On the profit calculator, you will type in the price you want to sell the product for on Amazon. You then will then need type in what you will pay for it at the thrift store. Then add in the Amazon fees that they will charge you and the cost it will be to ship the item to the customer. This app will calculate your total profit which is the most important number to know after all is said and done.

For instance: you buy a book at the thrift store for $3 and sell it for $20

Profit calculator:
$20 (sell price) - $3 (buy cost)= $17
$17- $6 (Amazon seller fee)= $11
$11-$4 (to ship book to customer)= $7

Profit=$7

So you just turned $3 into $7. Sure there were fees you had to pay and shipping costs you had to add. But you can do this again and again. Your multiplying your money that's how the profit comes. You'll do this with the eBay profit calculator as well. It is similar to the Amazon calculator and you'll get your net profit results.

How Much To Spend On Each Item?

When most people start out selling items from thrift stores they will buy the cheapest items they can. They often won't spend more than a dollar or two. This is an okay strategy to use when starting out because you might not be comfortable with your skills and strategies, plus you will not want to spend too much money and lose it.

In the long-term, you will want to buy items that are priced up to $10 or more. The reason for this is that at thrift stores everybody is looking for those one or two dollar deals. Also, when you buy something for a dollar or two sometimes you can only sell it for $10 or $15 and you will make a small profit.

This is okay, but what I want to tell you is that the big money is on the items that are higher-priced.

For instance, you might see an item that is selling for $12.99. Because it's priced at $12.99 in a thrift store many people might overlook it thinking that it's a high priced item. But they might not realize is that this item might be selling for $60 or more on Amazon and eBay.

If you were to sell it for $60 you would make a cool profit of $35 after shipping and seller fees are added. If you continue to do this with the higher-priced items, you would reach your goal of $1,000 pretty quick. My advice would be to always look for the best deal which you can flip for a high profit. Don't worry about buying the cheapest item all the time.

Items to Buy and Categories

Books are my favorite item to find. The reason for this is that they're almost always priced $3 or below and there is potential that a book might be worth up to $100, sometimes even more.

Not all books will sell at that price and 95 per percent of the books in every thrift store are not really good to sell for-profit. You will have to use your scouting app to see how much the books are selling for online.

You need to know that non-fiction books, especially educational or textbooks will sell for the highest price.

Try to stay away from fiction books and for the most part. Also stay clear of children's books because they usually don't have much resale value. Many textbooks have a retail price of $100 or more and most nonfiction books have a retail price over $25+ that gives you room to resell them at a high price.

Another good thing about books this is that its value doesn't jump out at you right away. Most people will often overlook high-value books and never even understand the value. This is where you come in and pick it up.

Media Items Such as CDs DVDs and VHS, as well as Cassettes

Media items are hot sellers at thrift stores. This is because they are small and sell at low prices. They are sort of an impulse buy. Some of these can be quite rare in demand for high-priced online at eBay or Amazon.

As you continue to scout at thrift stores and learn about the pricing of these items you'll get a better feel and eye for spotting the gems. Many times the most popular or well-known media items aren't always the best in terms of profit value.

The more well-known a CD or DVD is the more there will be available of these on the secondary Market. This means that many people have given these away to thrift stores or gotten rid of them and since you're such a plethora of them available the price online is pretty low.

For instance, a Titanic movie DVD which was very popular and came out a few years ago. Thousands upon thousands of them were sold and many people got rid of it and don't want it anymore. It's probably also available in places such as Netflix because it's so popular. So supply outweighs demand at this point.

On the flip side of that, if you can find a rare DVD on dog training. Since not many places have it you will become one of the sole sellers of it on Amazon. Tha hat means you can price high, and the person buying it will be willing to pay that price.

You'll do this with many of your media items. Then you'll soon come to find out that the more rare or obscure the niche, the more likelihood it will have a good profit potential.

If it's something that you've never heard of, it might be likely that it's rare and someone wants it online.

Some media items such as VHS, vinyl records, and cassette are still being sold at thrift stores. Your first thought would be that no one would ever want to purchase these because they are outdated and worthless. That's a good conclusion to draw but one that isn't exactly true.

The strange but cool thing is that VHS and cassette are sold consistently on Amazon and eBay. Of course, most of what is being sold in thrift stores from these outdated media types are not worth anything to resell. But if you get a good eye for what is profitable which you will begin to acquire more practice, you will start to see patterns of what could still sell for profit.

For instance, on VHS there are many movies that were made many years ago that never got put on DVD for whatever reason. If someone wants to watch that movie but it isn't on DVD, they will have to buy it on VHS. They will look on Amazon for the movie and see you selling it. They will then buy it from you. Hopefully at a price that is high because you might have the only one that's available anywhere.

Also, some music connoisseurs want to buy vinyl records for their collections. It might not be the most popular medium but it is a medium that is still relevant to some so you might still be able to sell music cassettes and vinyl records that are in demand.

Clothing

Used clothing that you find at thrift stores, for the most part, will only be able to be sold on eBay. You won't be allowed to sell it on Amazon because of Amazon's standards.

A good tip to know is that any brand that is sold for a very high price might be a good pickup at a thrift store. Brands such as Polo Ralph Lauren, Coach, Prada, etc. Things that are not a luxury name brand are usually a tough sell on eBay and won't be worth your while.

The good news is that there are lots of sellers on eBay that have paved the way and continue to make good money selling clothes online that they find at thrift stores.

You might want to check out YouTube for people that sell clothes on eBay. They often have many good tutorials and educational videos that boast in a good way of what they sold recently. They will show you things such as shoes, purses, suits, dress shirts, ties, and other clothing items that they flip for good profit. This can be tough sometimes though.

This is because people are pretty well aware of brands and when they see luxury ite in a thrift store they usually will buy them pretty quickly which will not be good for you. Also, thrift stores have become more and more aware that these high demand and luxury brands are part of their inventory. So they often mark up the price and when they do this, they cut into your profit potential.

For instance, a thrift store might sell most of their jackets for $5.99. They might have a nice Ralph Lauren jacket, and since they know it's Ralph Lauren, will mark it up to $19.99. The jacket might actually be worth $35 on eBay. But since they marked up the price so high you might not have any profit potential.

The thing is though, maybe that Ralph Lauren jacket is worth $100. If it's a good seller, would I buy it at $19.99? Yes, I would it and it would bring me for sure $60 profit. So you just going to have to learn how to navigate and see what is a good deal and what isn't.

A word of warning is that anything that is common and not name brand, is usually never a good thing to buy at a thrift store because the resale value will never be much more than what the thrift store is selling it for. Let's say a Dockers dress shirt is selling for $5.99 at Goodwill. That's probably what it's worth and you wouldn't get any more for it on the internet.

Board Games

Board games are great because they're almost always sold at a low price. What's weird though is that there are so many new ones that you can find the thrift store.

I'm not sure why there are so many new ones available but that's a good thing because anything new can be priced higher than something that is used. Board games are usually never priced more than $5. You would be surprised though how much you can get by selling them.

Depending on if it's new or if it's rare or in high demand that will set the price point. When your game is new there is a high chance you can sell it for $20 and more. If a board game is in high demand or rare it also could be $20 or more. The best deals are the deals were the board game is new plus it is in high demand or that's when you can make $25 or more on it.

If you are selling board games make sure that you always have all the pieces and nothing is missing.

Toys

Toys are very plentiful at thrift stores from action figures to dolls, video games and small handheld video systems. Toys are one of the main things that are brought to thrift stores when the kids no longer play with them.

The good thing about toys is that they remain in demand even as time passes. Sometimes kids lose their favorite toy and want to buy it again and they can't find it in the store so their parents have to buy it on the internet even when it is used.

Sometimes even grown-ups want to buy toys. Grown-ups that had a toy long ago might want to repurchase it again either for their children or to remind them of when they were a kid. If they see it on Amazon or Ebay used deal probably pick it up. I once found a huge lot new poker handheld video games. They were being sold for about $5 or maybe $4. I was able to pick up about 30 of them. On Amazon, I sold most of them for at least $60 each.

Stuffed Animals

Stuffed animals are one of the Hidden gems at thrift stores. If you're going to sell them you got to make sure that there in presentable condition especially if you're going to sell them on Amazon. I would never sell a stuffed animal that wasn't in at least good condition with no stains.

Often stuffed animals are made in the form of different characters such as Winnie the Pooh

Donald Duck, or Mickey Mouse. Each one has a different design and size.

Look for the characters that are well-known or even ones that are well-known but aren't exactly made a very often.

Think of a well-known Disney character in a movie that came out about 20 years ago. You might find plush of that character. There's a good chance that it can be sold on the internet for a high price because you'll probably get it for $1 or $2.

Many stuffed animals can sell for $20 or more. Some stuffed animals are just generic and not name brand these usually won't fetch much of anything. So that it is to get them cheaply and focus on well-known characters especially plush stuffed animals that are a bit oversized because usually will have a high value.

New Items

I pay very close attention to anything that is new that I can find at thrifts. Some are new, still in the package, and over 20 years old. I'm often suprised how many old school, sealed items that can be found at thrift stores. Where all these items coming from I have no idea.

Sometimes I find things that are very old and they're still sealed, such as a whole case of brand new blank VHS tapes. Maybe these tapes were owned by a store in which the store owner closed many years ago and they kept old inventory in their house?

They finally ended up giving them to the thrift store. Now you have a vintage item that is still very sellable and in demand.

Know that some things that are brand new can also sometimes be pretty worthless and outdated. You might find a bunch of old cell phone cases of for cell phones that were popular up to 10 years ago. No matter how hard you try people aren't going to buy those even though they're brand new and sealed, so keep that in mind.

Some stores such as Target sell some of their brand new items that didn't end up selling, at thrift stores like Goodwill.

Actually, I'm not sure if they actually sell them to Goodwill at a cheap price or just give them away to Goodwill. In any case, you can find a lot of sealed items from Target at Goodwill. These might be sellable for a good price.

Other Items

There are many many other items that thrift stores might sell. I'm not going to list them all because there are so many different categories.

Because you will run into all sorts of random stuff, over time you'll get a better understanding what has value or might have value.

One example is coffee mugs. There are some coffee mugs that can fetch over $20 each. That's not one of my specialties, so I have some trouble figuring out which ones are collectible and which ones are not. As you search and find more thrift store items, you will get better and better at spotting the best deals.

Selling in Bundles or Sets

Sometimes things that don't sell very well individually will sell a lot better if they're sold as a set.

Let's just say you have a book by Joyce Meyer, a popular author that sells well on eBay. Or even a book by Robert Kiyosaki, the author of Rich Dad Poor Dad. Individual books by these two authors don't bring much money because they're only worth $4 individually.

But if you're able to get quite a few books by these two authors it might work good in a set. I went collected quite a few different books by Robert Kiyosaki maybe around 25 different titles in his Rich Dad Poor Dad series. I ended up being able to sell this these as a set for $150.
The purchase price on them was about a dollar each to bring it to about a $25 cost. I shipped it through Media Mail which was about $20 or so plus my eBay fees.

I ended up getting about a hundred bucks profit.

Joyce Meyer books won't make you much individually but if you can find 20 books by her you might be able to sell it for a hundred bucks as well and make $60 or $70. Of course, you have to be patient with this and it takes more time, but it's another option you can use.

You also could do different categories of books as a bundle or set on eBay such as a group of books on cooking or a group of books on sewing. Or maybe you have a bunch of different legos that you purchased at thrift stores, you might be able to throw them into a big lot and sell it.

On Amazon, it is a bit different. You can't just throw up whatever you want and list it because they're a bit more strict than that on Amazon. If you look up something on Amazon and you'll have to sell exactly what is listed there. You can't just throw a bunch of different books on their haphazardly or the way you want to do it. eBay will allow you to that though.

So, for the most part, this strategy will work pretty much work on eBay.

What Not to Buy

There are many items that might not be worth selling. Especially those that are oversized and are hard to ship. Many large items are pretty much impossible to ship at a cheap price. Which leads to them being items you don't want to buy.

Items such as furniture, computers that are large, as well as TVs, usually cost more to ship then they're actually even worth themselves. You always need to factor in how heavy and item is in some cases and how large it is.

When an item is too hard to ship and very heavy even though it's a great item, you might not be able to make money on it.

Also stay clear of anything that's heavily damaged or broken or missing parts. Unless you know that the item is something that people will buy for parts on eBay don't buy it. Items that are heavily damaged or broken are not sellable on Amazon because of their standards.

Items That Can Be Sold and Flipped on Craigslist

One exception to the rule of not buying large items is buying items that you can sell on Craigslist. For instance, see you saw a very large nice massage chair at a thrift.

You might spot amassage chair that you might see for $1,000 or more brand new. Somehow you see they're selling it for $75 in good condition. You might just know that you can sell it for way more than that maybe even sell it and flip it quick for 300 dollars.

Your only real option might be Craigslist, which would be your best option. You might want to pick that up and do a quick flip on Craigslist even though you won't be able to sell it on an online platform because the item is just too big.

Keep in mind though that every time you deal with large items you need to be able to pick it up from the thrift store bring it to your house, It'll take up extra space to store it. If you don't sell it quickly it might take up a lot of space in your house and you might end up flipping it for barely any profit anyway.

For me, I wouldn't do this too much unless I knew I could flip it very quickly and that it would bring a good profit guaranteed.

Another item you might buy might be a bicycle that sells for $500 on the used Market. If you can pick it up for a hundred bucks and you know that you can make a hundred or $200 profit at least, It might be totally worth it to do it.

It's all up to you and what you're comfortable with.

Section 3. More important facts to know

Shipping

One of the most over looked parts of a thrift store reselling operation is shipping costs. If you are good at shipping and can ship the right way, you really increase your profits.
If you don't have a good plan or learn the basics. Or quickly learn some of the tricks of shipping items to customers, you will lose out on a lot of money.

Always remember that the lower you can pay to ship an item, the more profit you receive. This is because it's another expense you don't have to pay. It might seem like common sense but sometimes we overlook it.

One of the things thats great is that USPS or the United States Postal Service gives free boxes that are called flat rate boxes. They will allow you to ship you're an item for a flat rate.

For instance, one flat rate box costs about $6 and it would arrive in about three days time. In this box, you might be able to send a cell phone or something similar in size.

Another box cost about $19 and his big enough to hold a a very large DVD player. The good thing about these boxes as anything that fits will ship for that flat rate even if it's very heavy.
There's also something called first class mail. This is for items that weigh less than 13 ounces. First class mail ships from $2 all the way up to around $5 or so. There's also standard post which ships for a rate that is lower than Priority Flat Rate boxes if the item isn't too heavy.

One really cool thing that you want to take advantage of is that anything that is a media item such as books, CDs, DVDs, cassette etc. are given a discount rate.

The discount rate is called media mail, and it only applies to items that are media items. They'll take a little bit more time to arrive than the other types of shipping options but they're usually very very cheap compared to the rest.

So in many cases, you want to ship your books CDs and DVDs another media items through media mail to really hike up your profits and profit margin.

Another good tip is that on the USPS site you can order free boxes that are flat rate boxes and have them shipped to your house. They also have boxes and special envelopes that are a flat rate which available on the USPS site.

One hidden secret is called the flat rate padded envelope. Anything that fits in here costs just under $7, even if it's pretty heavy.

I consider this envelope my secret weapon because many times I saved a boatload of money because I ship something very heavy that was pretty big in the $7 envelope.

They also have a board game sized flat rate box as well as a box that is made to ship shoes flat rate. Again these three types of boxes are only available on the USPS site and you have to order it online but they are free.

You might be pretty confused by all the shipping options, but it's just something you have to learn with time.

I gave you a good starting point and an outline of some of the basics of shipping, which I hope is of help.

Storing and housing your items and shipping supplies

When you first start out buying items to sell it might be cool because it'll take up not much of any space in your house. The better you get and sell, the more you buy the more you'll have to store. It's a good thing and a bad thing.

As you begin to overflow with items just because you're buying more and growing your operation, you'll have to think of a strategy to store your items.

One thing I do is I set up all my tools and shipping supplies neatly in a consistent area and keep them stored well. I also make sure that I store the items that I bought in a way that is not haphazard but is organized. Such as bins or boxes that are labeled.

Home improvement stores or Walmart usually has cheap shelving that you can put together in about 15 minutes or less. This can keep your stuff organized. I know some seller that buy large bins and they stock the bins with their different items that they're selling.

The key is to keep everything neat as you rotate stock you're buying and shipping. Know when to expand your area or your shelving or boxes. Because if you don't expand you will end up having a big mess that is hard to wade through and it becomes a burden to you.

Inventory

You can buy lots of items, but you need to make sure that they sell on a consistent basis. Not everything has to sell right away or very quickly.

You might notice that some items take months to sell. That is ok because many times that are the most expensive and profitable are priced up to $100 will take a long time to sell. This because you're looking for that one right buyer.

If you bought the item for $3 and you have to wait one year for the right buyer to give you $100 isn't it worth it to do it?

It can get ridiculous though if you have a bunch of stuff that just never sells or takes forever to sell. The strategy I used to have a mix of items that sell quickly, items that a little bit slower, and items that sell in a medium range time frame.
You can never really be sure how quick many items will sell, but you'll get better at figuring it out as time goes along.

Many times when I see a lot of my items not selling I will lower the price especially when I'm still going to make a pretty good profit. This is because when I lower it and give the people a good deal it will sell quickly and I'll put money back in my pocket with profit that will help me buy even more inventory.

Seasonal issues

There are twelve months and four seasons in a year.

What you might not know or understand is in the online selling world there are times and seasons as well.

On eBay, many sellers complain that summertime is unbelievably slow compared to other times of the year. Many sellers get fewer sales in the summer than they do around Christmas time or other times in the year.

I have found this to be personally true as well on eBay.

On Amazon, there's something called quarter 4. This is at Christmas time where Amazon Seller see an unusual and amazing spike in sales because everybody's in a buying mood because it's the Christmas season.

Sometimes as a seller, you will have days where you don't sell anything and then a week will go by where you have an unusually low amount of sales.

This might freak out and disturb you. If you haven't made bad decisions or done anything wrong the reason is probably that it's just a slow week and what you're selling might not be that relevant to buyers and that particular time or season.

For instance, on a certain holiday, I noticed that I wasn't getting much sales. This was because everybody was celebrating the holiday they were not home buying things online.

On that particular day or on certain holidays I don't get many sales and I expect that. Then the next day my sales went up again.

So just know that during some days and some times of the year you might not get many sales but hang in there and keep going because a big sale day is usually right around the corner.

Do keep in mind sometimes it is something that you need to adjust. I didn't get any sales for a couple days and I decided to lower the price on a few of my items.

This wasn't me freaking out but it was me seeing that I needed to make some sales and I needed some cash flow and I was willing to lower my price a bit in order to get it and quite a few items did start to sell.

Pricing

When pricing your items remember that you need to be competitive. On a platform like Amazon, you can usually charge a very good price.

When you list your item you don't always have to be there lowest price but priced competitively for the most part.

Just say that most of the sellers on Amazon are pricing a CD at $30. One particular person is selling it for $18.
If you're going to price your item today what would you do?

You might want to just place it around $30 because once that person sells their item at $18 you could be the next in line for a larger profit.

It all depends though because you might have bought the item for a dollar and you wouldn't mind making less if you can sell it quick.

In that situation, I would probably price at around $30. Just because that's probably what it's worth. The other guy at $18 is undervaluing and is losing money, You don't always want to give people that steal of a deal because in the long run that will cost you lots of money and you'll leave a lot of money on the table.

So just remember you're in the business of making a profit not just selling stuff. If I sold 1000 items but only made $3 profit on each of them I would only make $3,000.

If I sold 1000 items but sold them for a profit of $25 a piece I would make $25,000 you see the difference?

Sometimes it's better just to price high or very competitively and sell fewer items then to sell lots of items that you have at bargain-basement prices.

Sometimes an item will just be stuck on your shelf and not sell for months. You might get just sick and tired of looking at it. If you just adjusted the price a couple bucks you might sell it quickly and that might be the right thing to do. One time I was selling a certain item for about $79. I had plenty of them and I wanted to get the best price that I could.I figured that that was the going rate that others were selling it at.

The problem was I had the item posted on eBay weeks but they weren't selling. I might have sold one in a couple of weeks time. I picked up these items for about $6. I did want to get the most for my money and the most profit that I could, but I had about 10 of this particular item. I lowered the price to $59 which was still a great return and what happened was I ended up selling about one a day quickly.

Learning how often in item sells

One good thing about Amazon and eBay is you can actually track how often and how well items sell. On Amazon, they have a thing called sales rank.

If I was to look up the Titanic DVD on Amazon.com, The sales rank for the DVD might be 85,000. If I was to look up another DVD one that is more obscure the rank might be 600,000.

That will tell me that the Titanic DVD sells a lot more often than the other DVD, which means that I can for the most part bank on it selling much quicker than the other.

I wouldn't try to sell the titanic DVD though. That Titanic DVD might only be worth $4. I might end up buying it for $2 at the thrift store and since it's about to $2.50 to ship I would actually lose money on this deal, that doesn't even add in seller fees on eBay or Amazon.

The DVD ranked is 600,000 might actually be worth $50. Even though it might not sell for a couple months, it's still worth it to buy because I'll make over $35 after all is said and done. Not bad if I am only investing a buck or two.

The one thing you have to understand is that different categories of things on Amazon have different sales ranks.

Books have a certain sales rank under the book category. There are over 10 million books on Amazon, so if a book is ranked 500,000 it might be a pretty quick seller in the book category.

There are less than then 100,000 video games in existence on Amazon. That means if a video game is ranked 60,000 and you have a book that's right 500,000, the book is a much better seller. So we have to be sure that you know by looking at a sales rank chart or list that you can find on Amazon the best sales rank for each category.

Definately find and search for an Amazon sales rank chart to find sales ranks for different categories on Amazon.

Things are a bit different on eBay that actually might seem to be a little bit easier for those that are just beginning. The way you can tell if something is selling and is a good seller is called checking "completed listing". You can actually check to see how well a certain item sold in the not-so-distant past.

Let's just say you found a particular Wiggles DVD. You can actually type in the Wiggles DVD on eBay. You'll then see all the listings of that particular DVD that are currently available.

What you will do is click advanced search and Mark and check completed listings. What will happen is all the Wiggles DVDs of this particular title that have sold the last couple days weeks or months will pop up. It'll even show the ones that were purchased and those that didn't end up selling.

As you scroll through it you will see which ones sold and for what price they sold at that will be the price that you will probably end up having to sell the DVD at if you choose to buy it.

Let's just say this DVD sold a few times for $ 5. Also, look through the completed listings any see many of them didn't sell at all. From looking at this completed listing report you'll come to the conclusion that it's only selling for $5 which is not good at all.

Also, it's not really selling that consistently with many of them not being purchased.

You will not want to purchase this because you will not make much of any money on it and it doesn't sell well.

Let's just say you see another DVD which of the dog training DVD. You scroll through the completed items and you see that it's pretty rare so there were only four listings in the last 2 months.

But you see that three out of four of them sold for $45, $75, and $59. You then see that the one that didn't sell was being sold at $120. You now can come to the conclusion that this item will sell very consistently if you price it around $55 or so or even a little bit more. This would be a great purchase if you can pick it up cheaply.

You've done your research and you're no longer just guessing but you've educated yourself on it's worth.

Discounts

The great thing about thrift stores are discounts. Since these stores get items for basically next to nothing, they can be pretty generous on their thrift store sales and deals. Sales can happen every so often. Sometimes weekly or seasonally, it all depends. Some thrift stores have special deals on certain holidays. Some will have 50% off days.

Some thrift stores also have a certain day of the week that might be 25% off. You might have discounts for seniors at 25% off as well. Goodwill stores that I frequent often have a certain group of items that are half off every week.

Sometimes I won't purchase a certain item because I can't make enough profit on it, but once it hits 50% off level I might be able to really score on it.

For instance, a thrift might be selling DVDs for $3. but then they have a 50% off sale so I can purchase them for a dollar fifty instead. will be quite a few DVDs that I would not purchase at $3 but I would be more than willing to buy it for a dollar fifty because I'll be making a better and profit it's more worth my while.

Some of the thrift stores have discount cards where if you buy a certain number of items or spend a certain amount of mone, they give you a certain percentage off. Such as 30% off your next purchase. So you will want to add this strategy to your arsenal of thrift store sourcing.

I'll be speaking in next few paragraphs about creating a system that you can consistently do and scale up. This is where you'll see consistent income and growth in your profits that don't waiver.

Competition

You won't be the only one trying to score a deal. Everybody in a thrift store is there to get something for a great price and get a great deal.

You'll want to know on what days each thrift store usually puts out new items. The reason for this is often when stores replenish they will replenish on a certain day maybe it's a Monday or maybe Tuesday. This will be the day when most of the new stuff comes out.

If it's a great deal many people will want to buy top items right away and it might be gone within hours.

At some thrift stores, there won't be many profitable books for about a week and a half. Then suddenly on a Monday afternoon, whole new stacks of books come out with great profits. Sometimes another bookseller that is trying to resell on Amazon or eBay will come in and get first dibs on the books.

There is competition, but you need to make sure that you do not get too worried about it. Just continue to do what you can to find the best items to bring profit. Sometimes you need to get smarter than the competition and start learning about certain items that many people overlook.

Many people don't notice certain valuable products and items. You'll be able to score big if you begin finding hidden gems that many are overlooking.

Section 4. Creating a system

So you want to make $1,000 a month from thrift stores?

One of the things that have worked for me is creating a system. If you do thrifting randomly, you can only take it so far because you'll have times where you'll try to sell a lot of products. If you are not organized you may end up getting overwhelmed and quit. You might get frustrated because you have a full-time job but you just don't have the ability to really focus on your thrift store business in the right manner.

In the next couple paragraphs, I'm going to go over the steps that you're going to have to repeat over and over again thing.

This isn't a bad thing because the more you can automate the less stress you have. You'll also make more money and be more comfortable with what you are doing.

Sources and routes list

You're going to want to write down every single thrift store that you plan on frequenting on a weekly and monthly basis. You want to make a schedule on when you plan to hit the stores how often you plan to hit them and in what section of your community and area they are. The reason for this is you don't want to run like a chicken with your head cut off to different places at the wrong times.

It might be smart to source from thrift stores according to the general area they're located at. Do the north side on one day. Then on another day check out the south side of town. You also might want to make a plan on how you are going to look at garage sales and rummage sales if you plan on doing those as well. Plan on sourcing at the most lucrative places and spots the most.

This is because some thrift stores are better than others they have better quality goods at better prices. You will come to know which ones are good, which ones are great, and which ones are mediocre.

Listing schedule

You'll want to keep records of how much you bought each item for record keeping purposes.

You also need to have a time where you list the items either on Amazon or eBay.

This may take considerable time so you might want to batch this task and do it every so often. You also might want to have a time that you clean your items and get them prepped and ready.

When you list an item on Amazon it's actually pretty quick and you can get it done quickly which is great.

On eBay, it will take a lot longer. On eBay, you actually have to take pictures of your item give a description and a bunch of other stuff. This all takes a lot of time, but it is part of the process.

Listing your items on eBay is important as well. You'll probably want to do some research on the best ways to list items on eBay. One part of doing that is having a great picture or pictures for your listing.

This could involve having the proper setup to take pictures as well as having a very good camera and method of taking pictures of your items.

My advice would be to research on YouTube and also any other books or resources online that would tell you how to optimize your listing to make them more likely to sell.

Purchasing supplies

You need supplies such as tape, boxes, and mailing envelopes. I like to purchase these on Amazon.com especially with the Prime program. You can order these ever so often and keep tabs on what you need.

Another good place to purchase boxes at Home Depot or Walmart. Remember to take advantage of the free Priority Mail flat rate envelopes and boxes that USPS provides.

Have a list of all the supplies you need look up over it maybe every 2 to 3 weeks. Then order supplies in batches every so often.

Shipping your items

One thing that you'll need to do often is ship the items that you sell. You're going to want to make sure that you ship your items consistently. At least every other day.

The reason for this is that when you ship an item on Amazon they're pretty strict and ask you to ship not soon after the item was purchased by the buyer. Also on eBay, you will want to ship pretty soon after the buyer purchases as well.

You'll have less hassle and fewer buyers question you on where their order is because of late shipping.

You can either buy your postage on the computer or do it at the post office. It's up to you.

There used to be many discounts if you purchase your postage on the computer. There are fewer discounts available now than in the past.

Dealing with customers questions and returns

When you ship your items not everything will go smoothly 100% of the time this is just a fact of life.

Of course, you want to keep customer satisfaction at a high level. You'll do this by improving your game and learning things that satisfy the customer such as shipping in a better way making sure you pack items well and ship on time.

You can't satisfy every customer but you want to strive for as close to 100% as possible. On the Amazon and eBay platform, you're actually rated and graded as a merchant on these platforms. The goal for both Amazon and eBay is a hundred percent positice feedback rating.

Amazon and eBay use customer feedback to grade you and to keep tabs on how you are doing as a seller.

They sometimes sometimes give higher privileges to those that are rated closer to 100%.

If your ratings get too bad, warnings and even suspension of accounts could occur when you have multiple problems satisfying customers.

This often not be a problem if you're able to do things decently and in order.

You will make mistakes at times and you will be judged on those mistakes but all you can do is continue to learn and continue to get better and continue to satisfy customers.

If a customer gives you a bad feedback you might want to work with them to get it erased or to satisfy them in a way that would let them change their feedback score.

Sometimes you might ship the wrong item or you're item might not arrive even when you sent it accurately and correctly.

Try to respond to customers as soon as you can when they email you and be kind and courteous.

Refining

As you continue in learning how to sell and you get better at it, you'll start to find things that you enjoy selling and find worth your while.

You also find things that give you headaches and that you don't want to deal with. Of course there are headaches in every business opportunity and venture. Sometimes you just have to deal with them.

But often you will find a new way of doing things and avenues that you want to pursue. You might end up deciding for instance, that you only want to sell books and nothing else. I find bokselling easy to do.

Or you might say that clothing is your thing and that's all you want to sell. I think that if you are a part-timer focusing on only a few categories is the way to go.

This is because you have to learn a lot if you want to learn every category at a thrift store. You might not have the time or patience to do this,especially if you have a full-time job.

One of the things that I found out is that because of time constraints I needed to focus on items that give me a high-profit margin.

I started focusing on items sold for a profit of $20 or more. This is because I just didn't have the time to list and ship many items due to my schedule.

As I focused on the item that sold for a profit of $20 or more, I've actually gotten better at finding those types of products. It is true that whatever you focus on the most will grow.

You're in the business of making a profit not of just selling items. I ended up selling about half as much items, but almost made the same amount of profit. This is because I actually have gotten better at selling high ticket items.

Time

How much time do you want to spend on a thrift store business? The great thing is that it's up to you. You can walk into a thrift store anytime during the day and even after work. If you choose not to go today or for a whole week that might be fine as well in some cases.

You need to work smarter and not harder because that's a big part of this whole thrift store reselling game. You might have really wanted to get into it because you want a little bit extra money to improve your quality of life.

Not start another thing that's going to weigh on you and bring you down.

Whenever thrifting gets to be more of a curse than a blessing that's when you have to think about what you're doing and how you're operating.

One of my favorite books is a 4 Hour Work Week by Tim Ferriss. He went over the popular principle called the 80-20 Pareto Principle. What this is, is 80% of the good, as well as profits, come from 20% of what you do. So if you can find out what really works for you and for your lifestyle you might be able to work better in lot less time while making a good amount of income. With any business, there's going to be some struggle and a learning curve that you need to adjust to as well.

But remember the end of this should be that you're enjoying it and getting some extra cash. Thrifting should be a great addition to your life instead of something that is a pain in the neck.

Scaling Up

One of the things that I've done in thrifting is refine consistently until I have created a system that I want. That means selling the items I want and creating a system that works for me.

You can make more money than $1,000 a month. I believe that's just a foundation that you can get to quickly just following the advice on this book. If you want you can make a lot more money.

You will have to get better and better at spotting deals, as well as picking up products that give you a very high-profit margin. To scale up your business and make it larger, you will have to do one of two things.

Either you'll have to decide that you're going to sell more items than you are currently. This will also involve really refining your system and your routine in order to do things more efficiently.

Of course, it'll probably mean you'll spend more time on it then if you are when you're only making $1000 a month.

Another thing that you might want to do is really make your system more efficient. Focus on selling the things that really bring in the profits. Especially try selling the high ticket items ($25+ profit per sale).

The full-time reseller

The amazing thing is there are people that make a full-time income buying things from places like thrift stores. Many of these people have been doing it for years and years that are experts on finding deals and the right products to sell.

You can learn many tricks of the trade from them, especially on places like YouTube where they actually produce videos giving tips and insight into what they do. You always want to learn and gain knowledge and insight on your own. But it's also good to learn from others, because they can give you direction and new insights into things you might not figure out yourself. Or cutting edge tips that you can get moving in the right direction.

I would advise you to look up on and subscribe to any YouTube channels that are very popular and talk about selling items from thrift stores. You might also want to go to iTunes and look up any podcasts that are thrifting related.

You might think its unrealistic that you'll become a full-time reseller. That's fine.

I believe selling things from thrift stores is one of the great starting points to learning how to make extra money and income.

There's a lot of money to be made online and many opportunities that you can get into. By selling on eBay and Amazon you learn a lot of things about making money. Plus buying, selling, and dealing with customers. You can use this experience to grow into other business ventures.

I personally started just thrifting when I was younger. As I learn from it and also expanded into many other areas of business.

Section 5. Some more Specific items

Here I will give you a list help you get jump started. I will list and give a short overview of some of the items that are profitable. If you begin with this list you can get off to a good head start.

Textbooks
When looking for textbooks at thrift stores my advice is to look for any textbooks that are 10 years old or less. Especially books that are less than 5 years old. If a textbook less than 5 years old there's a good chance that it has very good value.

Textbooks are one of the most lucrative items at thrift stores. This is because brand new, they often cost $100 or more. The newer it is the more relevant it is, the more a textbook could be worth. The thing is, they are often lumped in with all the other books on the shelf and the average thrift store buyer isn't paying particularly good attention to them. Always look for textbooks.

Non-Fiction Books

There are many non-fiction books available at thrift stores and not all of them have any value when you sell them online. At least they don't have enough value to give you the profit that will make it worth your while.

Look for any books that are of a newer variety. Especially books that are academic or are in a special field of learning and knowledge. You should look for any book title or book that is about a subject that seems complicated with big words. It might be worth big bucks.

Of course, there's a lot of other non-fiction books that are mass-marketed.

A self-help book by Montel Williams, worthless.

A book by Dr. Laura Schlessinger from 1991, worthless.

Just about anything that's been mass marketed and has passed its day of relevancy isn't a good purchase or buy.

Used Electronics

When looking for used electronics you need to make sure everything is working and all the parts are there. The reason for this is that electronics are one of the items that often get returned because they don't meet the demands of the buyer and they are missing parts or don't work correctly.

I once sold a nice calculator. Little did I know that one of the buttons wasn't working. I mean I don't think I could ever figure that out unless I spent an extra 5 to 10 minutes pressing every button. But you see what I mean here. Electronics can bring a good profit margin as long as they're not too big to ship and everything is working.

Here's a good tip any electronic item that costs as much to ship as it's worth is probably not a good deal. For instance, you see a nice boombox that you can sell for $30. If it cost $30 to ship it, you're probably not going to make any profit. That's because the shipping will be ridiculous. See, you're going to want to go for the smaller electronic items that you can fit in a flat rate box that's not too expensive.

Sometimes an item might cost $30 or $40 to ship. If you can sell it for a high price say $100, you might make a good profit if you only end up buying it for $10 or less.

My advice is to look for any handheld electronic games, walkman, electronics item that you can sell for $30 to $50.If yu are able to pick up for $5 or $10 that will make you a good profit margin. The good thing is electronics are always plentiful in thrift stores.

CD and DVD Courses

Just a few days ago sold a course that I bought at a thrift store for $70. I remember purchasing this for $10. It did take a couple months to sell. It was well worth it because I'm figuring I made $50 profit.

CD and DVD courses and self-help type sets on topics such as real estate, dating, or just about any educational topics you can think of can have great resale value.

During this past week I sold a brand new course which was a DVD course I found still sealed at Goodwill. I bought it for about $3. it was worth over a $140 brand new.
I ended up listing it for about $100 and it sold quickly. I sold it a bit below market value because wanted to get the quick sale.

This shows the profitability of CD/DVD courses. These are usually set that are multi-disc and sell brand new for $100. The thrift stores might price them for $10 or less. You can see the profitability here.

Coffee Mugs

Coffee mugs are interesting because there are so many different kinds. Although many don't have any real value if resold. Quite a few are mass produced but some are rare.

I once found a nice red CNN coffee mug. The funny thing was I don't even sure how I knew, but that instinct kicked in and I just knew that it was valuable. I listed it on Amazon.com for around $70. It sold within a couple days. I had purchased it for under $5.

Shoes

Premium brand shoes in good condition are sold at thrift stores. They're usually priced around $10 or so, depending on the brand and the condition.

Some shoes brand new sell for $100-$200. What you want to do is find those brands and types of shoes that sell brand new at a very high price. You often can get at least half of the brand new price depending if it's in good condition. You have to remember shoes are pretty big. You will have to figure in shipping costs if you're trying to make money off of them.

Suits
Many brand name suits are sold at thrift stores. These can be brand new with price tags of hundreds of dollars when they are originally sold. The thrift store might be selling them for a low price.

Of course, you often won't get full price for suits, which you can only sell on eBay not Amazon. But if you can get them for a low enough price you can make a good profit.